New

FOWLER
PROFICIENCY

WRITING
SKILLS 1

W. S. FOWLER

SARAH BIDELEUX   GILL MACKIE

NEW EDITIONS
English Language Teaching

First published by New Editions 2002

New Editions
37 Bagley Wood Road
Kennington
Oxford OX1 5LY
England

New Editions
PO Box 76101
17110 Nea Smyrni
Athens
Greece

Tel: (+3) 010 9883156
Fax: (+3) 010 9880223
E-mail: enquiries@new-editions.com
Website: www.new-editions.com

© New Editions 2002

ISBN 960-8136-73-3   Student's Book
ISBN 960-8136-74-1   Teacher's Book

Every effort has been made to trace copyright holders. If any have been inadvertently overlooked, the publishers will be pleased to make the necessary acknowledgements at the first opportunity.

INTRODUCTION

New Fowler Proficiency Writing Skills 1 is the first part of a two-part course which aims to teach the techniques students require to attempt any of the variations among the six forms of writing task set in the revised Cambridge Proficiency examination. Approximately one third of the material in *Writing Skills* has been revised for this book. All the other material in this book is new. Eleven of the twenty units consist of two facing pages, and should, under normal circumstances, be completed in a lesson, with a writing task to be done later in approximately one hour, the time allowed for it in the examination. In the remaining nine units of four pages, two lessons will normally be required.

The changes in the examination

The biggest change in the writing paper of the revised Cambridge Proficiency examination is that it now has two parts, as do FCE and CAE.

Part 1 consists of a compulsory question comprising instructions and a text or texts which provide candidates with a clear context. There is always more than one point to address in this question, and candidates should learn to identify these points and ensure that they cover them when writing. The question is discursive, and candidates are expected to write one of the following:

an article
an essay
a letter
a proposal

In **Part 2**, candidates choose one question comprising instructions which give candidates guidance to the context. In order to be successful in Part 2, candidates should be competent at narrating, analysing, hypothesising, describing, giving reasons, persuading, judging priorities, evaluating, making recommendations, giving information and summarising. Candidates are expected to write one of the following, from a choice of three:

an article
a letter
a proposal
a review
a report

For those candidates who have studied one of the three set texts, Question 5 consists of three questions, one for each of the set texts. Candidates are required to write one of the following:

an article
an essay
a letter
a review
a report

The time limit (2 hours) and length of writing tasks (300-350 words), remain unchanged.

Teaching writing skills

It is important for students to understand that while credit is given to Proficiency candidates for their use of structure and vocabulary, these are not the only considerations to be taken into account; organisation and the relevance of the answer to the task are at least equally important. Different writing tasks require specific techniques to deal with them, and such techniques can be taught effectively through models written within the capacity of a good student that can be analysed, imitated and practised. These models are supported with revision of the necessary grammatical structures and lexical items by means of accompanying exercises and the reference section and the appendix at the end.

Doing justice to oneself in an examination

The Proficiency examination requires a considerably more sophisticated use of English than First Certificate and the difference between these two levels is often underestimated by students. The difference, however, is not so much a matter of using more complicated structures or a wider range of vocabulary as of providing an answer relevant to the question, well organised in good, clear sentences and paragraphs. The range of questions open to the examiner is considerable, as indicated by the contents pages of this book, but learning the right technique to deal with each is half the battle. Therefore, it is recommended that students pay particular attention to the tips provided throughout the book. These consist of practical advice on what to do and what not to do in a given situation and should make it possible for students who take it to do justice to themselves in the exam.

Contents

Contents

Describing and narrating

In this article, Martin Fraser describes his return to a small town in England after an absence of 25 years. Read the article and complete the exercises that follow.

What a difference!

When I was a boy I used to spend a fortnight every summer with my aunt Elizabeth in Leabury, a small town in the Midlands. But twenty-five years ago she retired and moved to the seaside, and I did not return until I had to go there on business last week.

My aunt's house was on the outskirts of the town so I often used to ride out into the country on my bicycle. I would follow the London road for a mile or two and then branch off for a circular tour of the neighbouring villages, eventually finding my way back by the other main road. About a mile from home there was a small pond with ducks swimming on it. I used to stop there to watch them and skim stones across the water. Beyond the pond was Hayward's Farm, with cows grazing in the fields, and then I would come down the hill into the town and turn right into my aunt's road to complete the circuit.

There have obviously been changes since I was a boy but I was not prepared for many of those I saw last week. For one thing, the motorway that passes close to the town actually goes over two of the villages I used to ride to. As you come into Leabury, you no longer pass a farm with cows grazing in the fields. A vast housing estate stretches from the motorway to what used to be the outskirts.

The centre of the town has been entirely transformed. The old buildings have been knocked down and there is a big shopping centre with a multi-storey car park beside it. There are no family shops in the main street now, only the same offices, stores and fast-food restaurants you find everywhere. The old town used to have a character of its own but now it is like any other place in England.

On the way back, I went to see my aunt's old house, though I hardly recognised it at first. The present owners have painted it bright yellow so it looks like a big jar of mustard. I shook my head in disbelief and turned towards home. But just before I reached the motorway, I suddenly saw something familiar, a little pond with a wall round it, some ducks, and two boys skimming stones across the water. At least some things have not changed.

2 This article refers to four separate times:

> **A** 25 or more years ago, when the writer was a boy
> **B** last week, when he visited the town again
> **C** the present moment
> **D** some time or period of time in between his childhood and now

Study *Reference section 12* on page **68** and *Reference section 14* on page **69** and then answer these questions, writing the correct letter of time reference (A, B, C or D) in the space, as in the example.

Which period or periods are referred to in:

a the first sentence?   𝒜 ....

b the whole of the second paragraph?   ....

c the first sentence of the third paragraph?   .... and ....

d the description of the entry to the town?   ....

e the description in the fourth paragraph?   .... and ....

f the writer's comments in the last paragraph? .... and ....

Which tenses (present, present perfect or past) or forms (used to, would) does the writer use to deal with each period?

A .... , ... , ...

B ....

C ....

D ....

3 Look at the pictures of Athens and work with another member of the class to decide what changes have taken place in the period of 70 years between the times when the photographs were taken.

4 Write an article about changes that have taken place in one of the following in recent years:

a your neighbourhood

b a place where you went on holiday as a child

c a city or country you first visited many years ago and have seen again recently

Follow this plan of four stages (though there may be more than four paragraphs):

> 1 Introduction, indicating the place and your association with it
>
> 2 Description of the place as it used to be
>
> 3 Description of the place as it is now, emphasising changes that have occurred
>
> 4 Your reactions to these changes

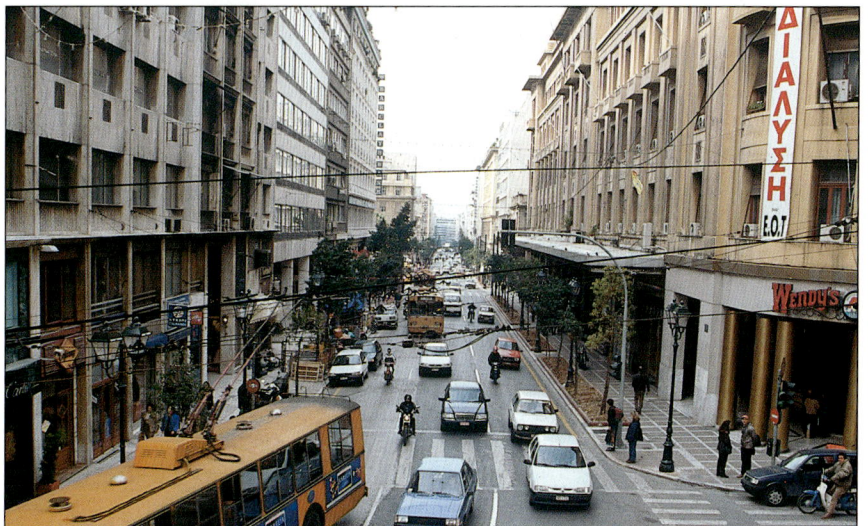

5 The description of changes in a place (pages 6-7) was told from the point of view of the present moment. In many articles of this kind, however, the main narrative tense is past.

Study *Reference section 12b* and *d* on page 68 and then read Gloria's article about a meeting with a school friend she met again after ten years who had changed. Most of the verbs have been left in brackets. Complete the article by putting them into the most suitable tense.

<u>Close friends again</u>

Soon after I left school my family (1) .... (move) to Bristol and I (2) .... (lose) touch with all my friends. When I (3) .... (return) to London last year after ten years, I (4) .... (find) some of their names in the phone book and we (5) .... (organise) a reunion. But there was no trace of Eugenia, my closest friend. The others told me they (6) .... (not see) her for a long time.

Eugenia was the most attractive girl in my class. She was tall and slim and (7) .... (have) lovely dark brown eyes and long black hair that (8) .... (come) half way down her back. She was very popular because she (9) .... (have) a wonderful sense of humour. She used to invent games to keep us all amused and always (10) .... (seem) to be laughing and smiling.

One morning last month I (11) .... (go) into a jeweller's shop in the city to buy a watch. The only assistant was a tall woman who (12) .... (look) a few years older than me. Her hair was grey and although she still (13) .... (have) a young, slim figure, there were lines around her eyes, and she (14) .... (have) a long, deep scar on her cheek. I (15) .... (ask) to see some watches, our eyes (16) .... (meet), and she (17) .... (give) a little cry of amazement. She (18) .... (stare) at me for a few seconds and then she (19) .... (say): "Gloria, (20) .... (you not remember) me?"

I (21) .... (shake) my head and her face (22) .... (grow) sad, but then she (23) .... (say) quietly: "No, I (24) .... (change) a lot, I suppose. I'm Eugenia."

I was so embarrassed that I (25) .... (not know) what to say so I just (26) .... (put) my arms round her. We (27) .... (arrange) to meet and then she (28) .... (tell) me the story of her life. She said that after leaving school, she (29) .... (go) to America and had married a man she had met there. They (30) .... (live) together happily for several years until her husband (31) .... (kill) in a car crash. She (32) .... (be) injured in the crash and her hair (33) .... (turn) grey overnight. After that she (34) .... (return) to London but (35) .... (have to) take the first job she could find.

I (36) .... (see) her several times since then. I want to do everything I can to help her. It was a terrible shock at first to see how much she (37) .... (change) but now we (38) .... (become) close friends again and can be together.

6 Gloria gives us a lot of information about herself and Eugenia. Find the paragraph in which she tells us the following and write the correct paragraph number in the space, as in the example.

a	how she lost contact with Eugenia	*1*
b	how she met her again	....
c	how she feels about her now	....
d	what Eugenia was like at school	....
e	what she looked like at school	....
f	what she used to do at school	....
g	what she does now	....
h	what she looks like now	....
i	what she was doing in the years between	....
j	where Gloria first met her	....
k	why Eugenia has changed	....

7 What do you think is the most important point in the story? Why? How does Gloria emphasise it?

8 Look at the pictures of the man and the woman and work with another member of the class to note down how they have changed physically in the course of thirty years.

9 Write an article with the main narrative tense in the past about the changes you noticed in someone you saw again not long ago but had not seen for a long time. The person may be someone you know or a famous person you saw in real life or on TV (not an actor/actress playing different parts).

Follow this plan of four stages (though there may be more than four paragraphs):

1 Introduction, indicating how you first saw the person

2 Description of what they used to look like If you knew them, what they were like; if you write about a famous person, say what impression they gave you.

3 Description of what they looked like when you saw them again, what they were like, or the impression they gave

4 Say how and why you think they had changed, and how you felt about the changes.

I Read the question and the article below and complete the exercises that follow.

The following comments were made during a public discussion, held at your town hall. The discussion was about the freedom of the press. You have been asked to write an article for the local newspaper responding to the comments and giving your own opinion.

> Journalists have a responsibility to the public to investigate a story and uncover the real facts – no matter who they upset.

> *You can't deny that a good scandal sells newspapers!*

> **They are encouraged to invade people's privacy by shameless celebrities who want press coverage at any cost.**

> *They should be ashamed of themselves! They have no respect for an individual's privacy!*

Journalists are fierce in defence of the freedom of the press but KEITH HUNTER asks

Whose freedom? Theirs or ours?

Every time there is an outcry against the excesses of the popular press and they are threatened with some kind of sanction, usually no more than the responsibility to print an apology where no one will notice it, editors and newspaper owners take refuge in the sacred concept of 'the freedom of the press' and warn against the evils of censorship. They argue that it is their duty to invade people's privacy, in effect to deprive them of their freedom to live their own lives in peace, because it is 'in the public interest.'

No one who believes in democracy and the freedom of speech wants newspapers to be silenced if they are genuinely engaged in exposing corruption in high places. In the newspapers' defence, it can also be argued that many figures in the public eye are desperate for almost any kind of publicity. Some of them seem to have no higher aim in life than a vague desire to feature in magazines, posing for photographs or recounting the intimate details of their lives in interviews.

Those who create news stories with sensational headlines, however, – the photographers who pursue the famous on motor cycles, the journalists who bribe their servants to disclose the secrets of their employers' private lives, the editors who send armies of employees with microphones and tape recorders to the home of anyone, rich or poor, whose relatives have died tragically – have a very clear aim in life. For them the freedom of the press is really the freedom to make money out of other people's shame and misery.

Most of us would be reluctant to impose censorship on the press but would like to put a stop to their intrusion into people's private lives. Not long ago there was a play on TV that suggested a neat solution. A Member of Parliament proposed that if a newspaper published an untrue story about someone, he would be given the same amount of space in the newspaper to write a story about the journalist or editor, true or false. I wonder how they would react if similar lies and half-truths about their own private lives and those of their families were published 'in the public interest'!

Tip

If you write an article where you are strongly in favour of something or against it, remember that others may have different opinions. It is more effective to mention them and then show they are wrong than not to mention them at all.

2   Choose the sentence, **a** or **b**, that best describes what the writer is saying in each paragraph. Then read the four correct sentences together to summarise the argument.

Paragraph 1   **a**   Editors are right to defend the freedom of the press when they are criticised.
                 b   Editors use the popular belief in the freedom of the press to justify their invasion of people's privacy. ....

Paragraph 2   **a**   No one wants censorship for political reasons and it is true that many well-known figures seek publicity at all costs.
                 b   Newspapers have a duty to expose corruption and have to publish stories about well-known figures if they are required to. ....

Paragraph 3   **a**   So newspapers work hard to find out the facts of the cases they investigate.
                 b   But newspapers only investigate stories about people's private lives to make money out of them. ....

Paragraph 4   **a**   Newspapers should be censored if they tell lies.
                 b   Newspaper staff should be subjected to the same treatment as their victims if they tell lies. ....

In which paragraphs is the writer following the technique suggested in the tip on the opposite page? ....

3   The writer tries to influence the reader with his choice of words. Answer the questions below to understand more about this.

a   Find words or phrases in the first two paragraphs that suggest the following:

The press
1   go too far in pursuing news stories.
....

2   are not really sorry for what they do.
....

3   are hypocritical in their defence of their actions.
....

4   upset people's lives.
....

Many well-known people
5   will do anything to be noticed.
....

6   have no serious aim in life.
....

7   invite the invasion of their privacy.
....

b   What is the effect of substituting these words for those the writer uses: follow (pursue), pay (bribe), information (secrets), numbers (armies), unhappiness (misery)?
....
....

c   Which of these words is obviously an exaggeration but effective because it also implies aggression?
....

4   Based on the composition and the tip on page 10, put the paragraph plan below into the correct order.

> **a**   Say why you disagree with these arguments and disregard them because those you support are more important. Give examples.   ....
>
> **b**   Reach a conclusion, summarising your personal opinion in two or three sentences.   ....
>
> **c**   Think of one or two ideas for the other side of the issue and say what sort of people are likely to support them.   ....
>
> **d**   Introduce the subject in general terms. Do not reach a conclusion immediately though you can suggest which side you are on.   ....

5   Look at this question and then put the paragraph notes below into the correct order according to the plan in exercise 4. Can you think of a suitable title?

You heard the following comments about vivisection while you attended a debate on the subject at college recently. You have decided to write an article for publication in the college magazine responding to these comments and giving your own opinion.

So many once fatal diseases are now curable and it's all thanks to research carried out on animals.

Under no circumstances should animals be used in laboratory experiments. Animals feel pain and shouldn't be made to suffer in this way.

Medical research is acceptable, but using animals for cosmetic testing is intolerable.

There is no justification for vivisection: animals have rights too.

Scientists – must carry out research on someone/something – better animals than humans. 1000s lives saved through medical breakthroughs – only possible because of experiments on animals. Humans are higher life form than animals – using animals justified.   ....

Conflict surrounding use of animals in labs – nothing new. Laws brought in – ban some experimentation. Extend law to cover ALL experiments?   ....

Medical research to save lives OK if NO other way of doing research possible. Cosmetic research not acceptable – total ban.   ....

Animal rights activists – all forms banned – no justification. Pain/Suffering extreme. Humans – no right to treat animals like this. Alternative methods must be found. Some research done for cosmetic reasons only!   ....

6   Choose one of the questions below and write your article using the paragraph plan opposite. Don't forget to think of a title.

a   You belong to a debating society and overheard these comments at a recent debate. The debate was about whether capital punishment should be restored for some crimes. You feel strongly about the issue and have decided to write an article for your local newspaper responding to the comments and giving your own opinion.

> An eye for an eye, a tooth for a tooth!

> *Taking another person's life is never right whatever the reason.*

> **If the restoration of capital punishment prevents even one murder, then it's worthwhile.**

> *What if someone who's innocent is found guilty?*

b   You live in a small town some of whose residents are becoming increasingly worried about sports and hobbies that harm the environment. The town council held a meeting to discuss the problem and you attended. After hearing what local people had to say, you decided to write an article for the local paper responding to the comments and giving your own opinion.

> *The quiet country lanes around the town are overrun with youths racing their motorbikes and creating a nuisance let alone putting the lives of others in danger.*

> The wildlife of Granger's Lake is being terrified every weekend by jet skis shattering the silence of this once peaceful haven. It's a disgrace.

> *If I can't ride my jet ski on the lake, where am I supposed to go?*

> **We live in this town too and should be able to do what we like, where and when we like. We're not breaking any laws.**

I Read the question and the article below and complete the exercises that follow.

Your tutor has shown you the following extracts on the subject of computers. You have been asked to write an article for the college magazine entitled *Computers: a dream or a nightmare?* Write your article taking the points raised below into consideration and giving your own opinion.

> *Technological progress in the world of computers saves everyone time. At the touch of a button, massive amounts of information can be accessed. Furthermore, work done on a computer can be updated and changes can be made speedily.*

> *Future generations will come to rely on computer technology to such a great extent that they will no longer need to learn to do things for themselves. This would appear to be acceptable, but what happens when the machines go wrong?*

Computers: a dream or a nightmare?

Within a few years, we have come to regard computers as an indispensable part of everyday life. We see them in operation in almost every office and they are increasingly common in the home. While this has been a great advantage for some people because it has made their work easier, it has been a nightmare for others, who have had difficulty in learning new skills. In the same way, while some parents believe that their children can learn faster with computers, others worry that they will become totally dependent on them before they have learnt to read, write and count for themselves.

On the one hand, the benefits computers have brought are obvious. Above all, they save space and time. Vast quantities of data can be kept economically on disks and reproduced at any time instead of filling rows of filing cabinets, and there are hundreds of time-consuming tasks that can now be performed very simply. In a minute or two, a typist can now edit and retype a letter; in a few seconds, a bank can check how much a customer has in an account in another city.

On the other hand, however, there are also disadvantages. Computers do make mistakes although they are always the result of a human error. We read of people receiving gas bills for millions of pounds because the computer has been badly programmed or an operator has pressed the wrong key. The trouble is that computers do not recognise such errors so there is a danger that the next generation may be taught to rely on them absolutely before they have learnt the basic skills necessary to work out problems for themselves.

On balance, computers are neither a dream nor a nightmare. They are admirable tools that improve the quality of life but, like all tools, they must be used sensibly. We must never forget that human beings provided them with the information they contain so we cannot trust them until we know enough to recognise when it is inaccurate. In this respect, the greatest risk comes at the national level; the advice given by a government computer could lead to disaster if those responsible for making the decisions were tempted to take it just because it came from a machine that is supposed to be infallible.

2 The writer's approach to the subject is balanced. Study *Connectors and Modifiers A3* on page 70 and underline the four words or phrases that the writer has used to balance his argument.

Tip

Good articles of this kind do not require the use of very complicated structures but they do require connectors to be well used. Always check the appendix on page 70 before writing one.

3 Answer these questions.

a Which two sentences in the first paragraph are examples of the writer balancing by using contrast. Which phrase does he use to show that he regards the examples as equal?

....

b What contrast exists between paragraphs 2 and 3?

....

c What conclusion does the writer reach? Is he in favour of computers or against them?

....

d Indicate the purpose of each paragraph, writing the correct number in the space.

Advantages of computers ....   Conclusion ....   Disadvantages ....   Introduction ....

4 The writer supports general statements with explanation or examples. Underline the phrases or sentences in the article that support these statements.

a We regard computers as an indispensable part of everyday life.
b For some people this has been an advantage, for others a nightmare.
c Computers save space.
d Computers save time.
e Computers make mistakes.
f The information they contain may not be correct.

5 A magazine is inviting readers to submit articles about different forms of transport. You have read the personal account below and have decided to write an article on the advantages and disadvantages of travelling by train. Write your article responding to the points below and giving your own opinion.

> *It seems that nowadays cars and aeroplanes are much more popular forms of transport than the train, depending, of course, on whether your journey is short or long distance. But I remember years ago, when I was a young child, that travelling by train was considered the best way to go.*

Before writing your article, look at the plan below and make some notes. You can write four paragraphs, following the same plan as the article on computers.

a Title. Think of a title for your article. While it is important for your article to have a suitable title, do not spend too much time on it.

b Introduction. Give a general impression of the current situation. Do not at this stage give explanations of advantages or disadvantages.

c Advantages of travelling by train. List three in comparison with cars or planes, and give an example or explanation for each, as in the table.

	Advantage	Example/Explanation
1	No traffic jams	difficult to calculate time of car journeys
2	....	....
3	....	....

d Disadvantages. List three disadvantages and give an explanation or example, as for paragraph 2.

	Disadvantage	Example/Explanation
1	....	....
2	....	....
3	....	....

e Conclusion. Sum up your argument, giving your own opinion.

1 Read the question below, the notes opposite and the article below, and complete the exercises that follow.

You belong to a society that is concerned about the environment. A guest speaker recently gave a talk to the society on the subject of the problem of population growth which you attended. You took some notes and have been asked to write an article for the society's monthly newspaper. Write your article.

World pop. doubled since 1950. UN predict + 50% by 2050.

World's natural resources – running out!

Impose birth control? – human rights/religion/tradition would not agree (eg China)

Politicians in developing countries say developed countries use too many resources – reduce, BUT still not a solution.

Put pressure on govts to find solution. If not = war, famine, disease!

Too many people, not enough earth

Of all the problems the human race is responsible for that threaten life on Earth, population growth is the most serious. The world's population has more than doubled since 1950 and the United Nations predict that it will grow a further 50% by 2050 to nine billion. All these additional people will require more food, more land to grow it on and more houses to live in, and will consume more raw materials to provide the basic requirements of everyday life. The world's resources cannot support such an increase indefinitely.

At first sight, the solution seems simple. Experts in developed countries argue that we should impose birth control worldwide. If parents only had the children they really wanted, they say, population growth would be manageable, as it is in Europe. People should be educated in reliable methods of birth control, and where necessary, these should be supplied. If a birth is not desired, the pregnancy should be terminated by abortion.

However, the failure of countries to reach agreement on problems like global warming indicates that there would be even stronger resistance if a plan of this kind were put into practice. In this case, the opposition would be due not merely to selfish national interests but to individual wishes and conviction, family or tribal tradition and the powerful influence of religious authorities. In some parts of the world, large families are considered desirable and a son is regarded as essential. In China, where the government has pursued a ruthless policy of limiting families to one child, population growth has only been controlled at the cost of considerable personal suffering.

Politicians in many developing countries, where the population is growing much faster than in Europe, refuse to accept that it is the main cause of environmental problems. They point out that countries like the United States consume far more than their fair share of the world's resources. Developed countries should reduce their consumption, but even if they did, this would not prevent disaster unless population growth was brought under control. We should put pressure on governments to find a viable solution. Otherwise, the painful alternative will become unavoidable; the population will eventually be decimated by war, famine and disease.

2 Choose the best heading for each paragraph, and write the correct number in the space. Note that two of the choices are not correct.

a	An alternative solution	....	**d**	Why a solution must be found	....
b	A straightforward solution	....	**e**	Selfish opposition	....
c	Why solutions are not easy	....	**f**	The size of the problem	....

3 Look at *Reference section 4a* and *b* on page 64 and *Reference section 11* on page 67 and then study the use of *should*, *would* and *will* in the article above and underline them where they appear.

4   Read Sarah's article on the environment. Complete it by putting the verbs in brackets in the correct tense or using *should* or *would* where necessary.

Preserving the planet for future generations

Human activity (1) .... (have) a devastating effect on the environment since the Industrial Revolution. Factories and their products have polluted the air in cities, and the water in rivers and seas; forests (2) .... (be transformed) into desert by poor methods of cultivation; in our hunger for land, we (3) .... (invade) the natural habitat of other species, now in danger of extinction. Our activities (4) .... (probably increase) the temperature of the earth, bringing with it the risk of flooding. What (5) .... (we do) to resolve these problems before it is too late?

Solutions certainly exist. In general, we (6) .... (consume) less and recycle raw materials. In particular, we (7) .... (restrict) the use of cars in cities; we (8) .... (close) factories that pollute the air or the rivers; we (9) .... (protect) wildlife by banning indiscriminate hunting; and we (10) .... (protect) the rainforests by providing poor farmers with the means to cultivate efficiently. Above all, we (11) .... (try) to control population growth, which (12) .... (add) to the problems as fast as we take steps to resolve them.

If we could accomplish this, we (13) .... (preserve) the planet for future generations. But it (14) .... (not be) possible unless governments laid aside self-interest and (15) .... (agree) to co-operate. In fact, laws protecting the environment already exist in almost every country. The trouble is that they are often broken, in many countries with the consent of the rulers. Perhaps a real solution (16) .... (only be found) if every country in the world had an honest, democratic government.

In such circumstances we may think that there is nothing we can do as individuals to save the environment. But we can do a great deal if we are prepared to make sacrifices. We (17) .... (ask) ourselves if we really need to go out in the car or buy something new. And we (18) .... (respect) the environment at all times. We (19) .... (not leave) litter around the countryside or throw rubbish in rivers. We (20) .... (plant) trees and not cut them down.

---

5   Sarah is following the same paragraph plan that was used for the article on population growth. In paragraphs 1, 2 and 4, circle the topic sentence and underline the examples that support it.

6   Write an article in answer to the question below, using the paragraph plan in exercise 2.

The extract below was taken from a letter you read in your college magazine. You have decided to write an article for the magazine responding to the letter and proposing some solutions to the problem.

… is just not the same any more. I remember walking along the river as a child and even swimming in it when the weather was warm. Now, the water is stagnant and polluted and the path along the bank is littered with rubbish.

The town centre itself has also been affected. Traffic blocks the roads and the poor pedestrians are choked with exhaust fumes. It really is time that something was done to save our town and the surrounding countryside before it's too late.

Tip

If you answer a problem-solving question, do not make vague general statements that you cannot support. Make use of any facts that you know to be true from what you have experienced or read. Take account of opposition to any solution you propose and bear in mind that there is probably no simple answer to the question.

Letters

Making suggestions

1 The local newspaper has offered prizes to readers making suggestions for improving the town where you live.

Read the letter from one of the older inhabitants of the town, published recently, and complete the exercises that follow.

Sir,

I am writing in response to your appeal for suggestions for improving our town. When I was young it was one of the most beautiful towns in the country, but its charm has been its downfall in recent years. It has been turned into a tourist attraction popular with young people who do not appreciate it. In consequence, most of the improvements I suggest would be attempts to preserve or restore what is left of this delightful place before it is destroyed.

One of the main problems is that air traffic to our tiny airport, especially cheap charter flights in summer arriving at night, has expanded to such an extent that those who live nearby are unable to sleep because of the noise. In my view the airport should be closed at night and tourist flights should be restricted to the hours of daylight.

It used to be very pleasant to walk through the narrow streets of the old town in the evening, with their restaurants and cafés, but now they have been replaced by bars and night clubs open till very late, playing loud music, and there are so many cars parked on the pavements that it is impossible to walk safely. The centre should be restored to its former attractive state. Bars should be required to close by 12.00 pm, the streets should be converted into a pedestrian precinct and a multi-storey car park should be built on the vacant site near the market.

Another useful innovation the council could introduce would be an information centre for tourists in the square outside the town hall. At present many visitors arrive without accommodation and wander through the streets in search of hotels and boarding houses, or stop passers-by to ask the way. If there were a properly equipped information centre, it would not only be of help to them but would be of great benefit to the tourist industry.

Alexander Martin

2 Read Mr Martin's letter again, and make notes about the problems he mentions and the solutions he suggests in the table below.

	Problem		Solution(s)
a	....	**1**	....
b	....	**2**	....
c	....	**3a**	....
		3b	....
d	....	**4**	....

3 Choose the best heading for each paragraph, and write the correct number in the space. Note that two of the choices are not correct.

a	A town for young people	....
b	Information for tourists	....
c	The airport	....
d	The newspaper's appeal	....
e	The old town	....
f	Tourists in the town	....

Tip

Note the form of address used to the editor of a newspaper, unless you know that she is a woman, in which case 'Madam' is used instead.

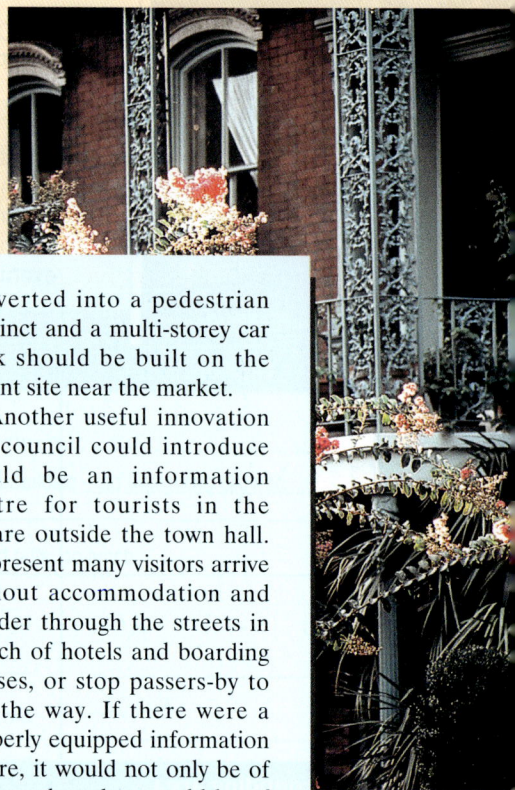

4 Young people usually have a different set of priorities from their parents and grandparents. Before you read Anna Margolis's letter, look at *Reference section 1* on page 64, *Reference section 11* on page 67 and *Reference section 13* on page 69. Now complete the letter by putting the verbs in brackets in the most appropriate form, using active or passive forms with *would, should, must* or *could*, and writing *the* or *a* in the spaces, <u>only where necessary</u>.

> Sir,
>
> While I agree with some of (1) .... suggestions (2) .... readers have made for improving (3) .... town, (4) .... main problem in my opinion is that (5) .... council is only concerned with attracting (6) .... tourists. In my view there are (7) .... number of improvements that (8) .... (undertake) for the benefit of (9) .... residents, especially (10) .... younger ones.
>
> In (11) .... first place, there are not enough sports and leisure facilities. Instead of building (12) .... multi-storey car park on (13) .... vacant site near (14) .... town centre, they (15) .... (construct) (16) .... indoor swimming pool and (17) .... tennis courts that (18) .... (use) in (19) .... winter.
>
> Secondly, I have read that (20) .... old railway station is going to be pulled down. The space (21) .... (transform) into (22) .... park and it (23) .... (not cost) much to provide a place for (24) .... small children to play (25) .... games. Part of it (26) .... (turn into) (27) .... adventure playground or (28) .... children's zoo.
>
> Lastly, tourists who go as far as (29) .... river (30) .... (disgust) by (31) .... litter along (32) .... banks and (33) .... pollution from (34) .... few old factories that are still in (35) .... operation. The area (36) .... (clean up), the factories (37) .... (close down) and (38) .... serious effort (39) .... (make) to transform (40) .... riverside area into (41) .... place where (42) .... people (43) .... (enjoy) (44) .... kind of pleasant walk they once had through (45) .... old part of (46) .... town.
>
> Anna Margolis

5 Anna lists three kinds of improvements, with a paragraph for each:

a introducing something new
b transforming something already in existence
c remedying something unsatisfactory

Complete the table below by referring to her letter.

	Problem		Solution(s)
a	Not enough leisure facilities	1	....
		2	....
b	Open space created when railway station is pulled down	3	....
		4a	....
		4b	....
c	Litter on river bank Pollution of river	5	....
		6	....

6 Write a letter addressed to the editor of your local newspaper, suggesting improvements that could be made to your town or the area of a city where you live. Follow the paragraph plan of Anna's letter and try to include at least one example of each kind of improvement.

I   Read the question and the letter below and complete the exercises that follow.

You have read the extract below as part of a letter to a local newspaper. You decide to write a letter to the same newspaper responding to the points raised and expressing your own views.

I know I am not alone in feeling threatened by the presence of groups of young people who seem to have nothing better to do than hang around the town centre making a nuisance of themselves. It is a reflection of our society nowadays: a society that encourages laziness and allows the younger generation to waste their time in this way. If something is not done soon, then I fear that these individuals will turn to crime and our town will no longer be the safe peaceful place it once was.

Sir,
    I am writing in response to a letter I read in Tuesday's edition of *The Kenton Herald* and have to say I feel the opinions expressed are a little one-sided in that the letter implies that young people are to be blamed for this situation and that it is what they want. It is my opinion that the community should accept some of the blame too. If solutions to this problem had been sought earlier, the situation might not have got so out of hand.

    While I admit that our town centre is increasingly a place where teenagers and young adults congregate, I also appreciate that many of them have no alternative. Young people have nowhere else to go. There are no youth clubs or centres in our area that could provide some form of occupation for them during the day. They are forced to either meet at each other's homes, often an impossible or undesirable option, or in public places, namely the town centre.

    In addition to this, it is well known that unemployment in our area is a serious problem among 18-25 year olds. Job opportunities are limited and any that are available are taken by people with qualifications or previous work experience. As a result, it has long been the case that if school leavers cannot go on to further education for whatever reason, they will be unlikely to find jobs locally. Moreover, there is the age-old problem: without experience, you can't get a job and if you can't get a job, how do you get experience?

    Finally, I am of the opinion that we should show more understanding towards these young people, who are, after all, our neighbours. Although it is unpleasant to see people hanging around on the streets, it must be even worse for those who are in this situation. If we were to offer them the chance to change their situation, I am sure they would do so. It is time for us all to take some responsibility for them and their position.

    I look forward to seeing my letter published in a forthcoming issue.

    John Holmes

2   Now read the letter again and answer the following questions.

In which paragraph(s) does John:

a   refer to the lack of facilities for young people?   ....
b   talk about whose responsibility the problem of young people on the streets is?   .... and ....
c   talk about unemployment being a reason for the situation?   ....
d   explain why he's writing?   ....
e   agree to some extent with what the writer of the letter in *The Kenton Herald* said?   ....

3   Look at these conditional sentences taken from the letter.

a   'If solutions to this problem had been sought earlier, the situation might not have got so out of hand.'
b   '... if school leavers cannot go on to further education ..., they will be unlikely to find jobs locally.'
c   'If we were to offer them the chance to change their situation, I am sure they would do so.'

Which one is an example of:

1   a present or future action in which the result will probably happen?   ....
2   a present or future action which is unlikely to happen   ....
3   a past action which cannot be changed?   ....

4   Look at *Reference section 4c* on page **64** and then write a conditional sentence to express the following situations.

a   Those boys didn't have jobs and spent their time doing a great
        deal of voluntary work.
        ....
        ....

b   This teenager was not offered the job so he didn't take it.
        ....
        ....

c   The police didn't allow young people to hang around on the
        streets in the past which is probably why they didn't do so.
        ....
        ....

d   There weren't groups of young people in the town centre years
        ago which meant people didn't feel threatened.
        ....
        ....

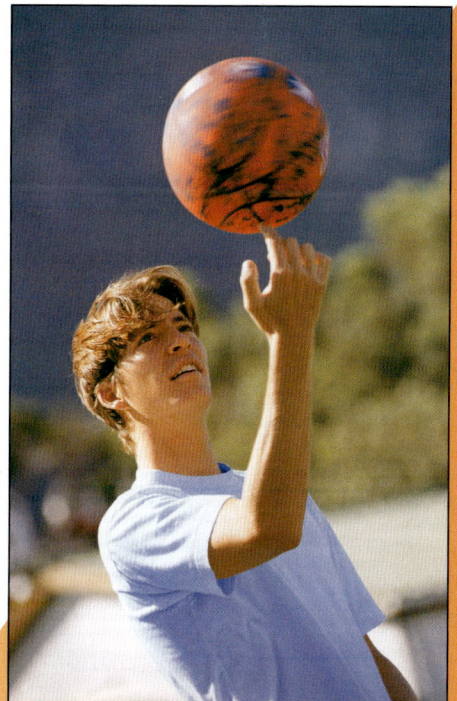

5 Now look at *Reference section 4e* on page 65. Look at how the conditional sentences from the letter can be rewritten.

    a 'If solutions to this problem had been sought earlier, the situation might not have got so out of hand.'

> Had solutions to this problem been sought earlier, the situation might not have got so out of hand.

    b 'If school leavers cannot go on to further education for whatever reason, they will be unlikely to find jobs locally.'

> Should school leavers be unable to go on to further education for whatever reason, they will be unlikely to find jobs locally.

    c 'If we were to offer them the chance to change their situation, I am sure they would do so.'

> Were we to offer them the chance to change their situation, I am sure they would do so.

6 Rewrite these sentences practising the more formal ways of writing conditional sentences.

    a If young people have no qualifications or training, they will not be able to find work.
    ....

    b If opportunities for training existed, I am sure people would take advantage of them.
    ....

    c If we all take an interest in our town, things will get better.
    ....

    d If teenagers had been encouraged to go on to college, they would have had better chances of finding work.
    ....
    ....

7   Look at this question below and then do the exercise which follows.

> You have read this extract about relationships between different generations in a national newspaper. You decide to write a letter to the same newspaper responding to the points mentioned and giving your own opinion.
>
> *I look at the younger generation now and can see no similarities with my own when we were young. Nowadays they have altogether too much freedom. They're encouraged to go out and see the world; to travel rather than settle down. Their priorities have changed. No longer do they want to raise a family: they're more interested in buying fast cars, expensive holidays and generally wasting their money. In my day we were expected to show respect to our elders, raise a family and become law abiding citizens.*

You will find it easier to answer this kind of question if you disagree with the points that have been raised in the extract. Answering these questions will help you to think of ideas to include in your letter.

a   The extract says that young people have 'too much' freedom. 'Too much' means 'more than they need or is good for them'. How can you support the alternative view that the freedom young people have is not excessive?

....

b   How have young people's priorities changed?

....

c   How can these changes be seen as a positive thing?

....

d   Is it true to say that young people 'no longer want to raise a family'?

....

e   What is the writer implying about young people today when he says: 'we were expected to show respect to our elders, raise a family and become law abiding citizens'?

....

8   Now use John's letter to help you organise your opinions into a paragraph plan and then write your letter.

9   Read the question below and, before you write your letter, ask yourself questions, as in exercise 7 above, to help you think of ideas.

> You have read the following extract in a magazine. You decide to write a letter to the same magazine responding to the points raised and giving your own opinions on the matter.
>
> *Things have really got out of hand. Everywhere you look there are pictures of skinny models who are supposed to represent perfect people. We're constantly told, directly or indirectly, that appearance is everything. Have we all forgotten that 'beauty is only skin deep'? Doesn't personality count for anything anymore? The cost of keeping fit and dressing fashionably is too high for the majority of people. Magazines, advertisements and the like should stop making ordinary people feel inferior.*

Tip

You don't have to disagree with everything that is said. You may agree to a certain extent but feel the opinions expressed are one-sided.

I Look at the question and the essay below and do the exercises that follow.

Your tutor shows you two extracts from articles about transport.

> *Working out which bus route is best and then waiting at stops for buses which are more often than not delayed or overcrowded is not my idea of fun. Nothing beats the convenience of being able to hop in my car and drive quickly to my destination.*

> *Public transport is better now than ever before. It's cheap, reliable and avoids the problem of finding or affording parking.*

Your tutor asks you to write an essay about public and private transport in the city, stating which form of transport you prefer.

(1) .... , the answer to the question 'Which is better in the city – public or private transport?' may seem obvious. Most people would rather use their own car than stand in a queue waiting for a bus. (2) .... , however, driving a car may not always be the most convenient form of transport in a city, even if the authorities allow you to take it into the centre.

Having your own form of transport, which usually means a car, naturally has advantages. (3) .... , at least (4) .... , is the fact that you can start and finish your journey when and where you like, driving from your house to your office, for example. (5) .... , (6) .... , even if you have your own parking space at home, you may find it difficult or expensive to park near your office. If that is the case, it would have been quicker and cheaper to travel by bus.

(7) .... , bus journeys are only quicker if the use of private cars is restricted because buses are likely to be held up in the same traffic jams. Provided you live near a bus route that takes you near your destination and the bus is on time, it is probably a better means of transport than your own car, but as we all know buses are often late and frequently crowded so you may have a very frustrating, uncomfortable journey.

When I was on holiday in London recently, I travelled in the centre of the city by taxi, bus and underground. The taxi fares were very expensive and the journey took a long time because the driver continually had to stop at traffic lights or behind a line of cars. The bus was even slower for the same reasons but also because it had to stop to pick up and set down passengers. The underground trains were crowded and uncomfortable but this was by far the fastest and cheapest way to cross the city. (8) .... , I would rather go by car than bus on the surface, but if I can travel underground in the city, I prefer public transport.

2 Study *Connectors and Modifiers* on page 70. Then read the essay again and complete it, choosing from the list of connecting phrases.

at first sight	*first and foremost*	*however*	*in fact*	*in practice*	*in theory*	*on the other hand*	*personally*

3 Answer these questions.

a Why is private transport preferable in theory?

....

b Why isn't it always better in practice?

....

c In what circumstances are journeys quicker by bus than by car?

....

d   Why are bus journeys often unreliable and unpleasant?

....

e   Why are journeys by bus usually slower than those by car?

....

f   Why are journeys by the underground the most convenient in central London?

....

4   Give each paragraph a heading, choosing from this list. Write the correct number in the space.

a	Advantages and disadvantages of travelling by bus	....
b	Advantages and disadvantages of travelling by car	....
c	Conclusion: it depends whether you are above ground	....
d	Introduction: is private transport always preferable?	....

> **Tip**
>
> *If you have to compare two things that each have advantages and disadvantages, it is easier to deal with them in separate paragraphs, concentrating on one at a time (see Paragraphs 2 and 3) than to write a number of sentences comparing them in the same paragraph.*

5   Read the question below, which is similar to the article you wrote in Unit 3 on travelling by train. There is a difference, however. There you were considering the good and bad points of one thing; here you are comparing two things with good and bad points in each case. Follow the same plan as the essay on the opposite page, using the notes below as a guide.

> Your class is going on a field trip to an island in the summer holidays. There has been much discussion about the best way to travel. Here are some of the comments that were made.
>
> *Flying is quicker, leaving us with more time to spend on our holiday.*
>
> *Travelling by boat is much more relaxing and gets you in the holiday mood before you get to the island.*
>
> *Think of the cost: flying is really expensive.*
>
> Your tutor has asked you to write an essay on this subject: *Which is the better way of travelling to an island, by sea or by air?* Write your essay, responding to the views expressed and stating your own preference.

a   Introduction. Write a balanced paragraph but do not go into too many details.

b   Explain the advantages and disadvantages of travelling by air. (But see TIP below)

c   Explain the advantages and disadvantages of travelling by sea.

d   Reach a conclusion. If you have a preference, say so and support it with an example, preferably from personal experience. If not, you can balance your conclusion, suggesting that the choice depends on factors such as the reason for the journey or the time of year etc. Give an example in each case.

> **Tip**
>
> *If you have to write an essay comparing two things, and have a strong preference for one of them, deal with the kind you prefer in paragraph 3 because it will lead more naturally into your conclusion. In this case, if you would rather go by air, reverse the order of paragraphs 2 and 3.*

I Read the question and the essay below and complete the exercises that follow.

> Your tutor shows you two extracts from articles about national character.

> *It is only natural that the climate affects people's personality. How can a worker from a hot country possibly work as hard as his northern counterpart? The same can be said for the happy-go-lucky attitude that so many people from warm places have, which is rarely seen in most colder countries.*

> *Assumptions that people have the same character simply because they are from the same country are completely unfounded. It is unfair to base opinions like this on what are, quite obviously, stereotypes.*

> Your tutor asks you to write an essay about the relation between national character and climate responding to the points raised and giving your own views on the matter. Write your essay.

Years ago, (1) .... historian Arnold Toynbee based his theory of (2) .... history on (3) .... climate. Comparing groups of immigrants to (4) .... United States, he argued that (5) .... Pilgrim Fathers in (6) .... New England were forced by their harsh climate to work hard and so became self-reliant and stern and puritanical in (7) .... temperament, while those who settled in (8) .... warmer southern states were easy-going and relaxed and depended on (9) .... slave labour. If his theory was correct, similar comparisons should be possible between the people of northern and southern Europe.

Needless to say, such generalisations cannot be applied to (10) .... individuals, and generalisations about people from different countries are based on stereotypes that foreigners form about them, which may be inaccurate or out of date. Some people in Greece may still imagine the typical Englishman as someone carrying (11) .... umbrella and wearing (12) .... bowler hat, even though the English tourists who come to Greece seldom remind anyone of this picture in their appearance or behaviour.

All the same, there is no doubt (13) .... grain of (14) .... truth in this theory that makes (15) .... sense. People from Scandinavia, historically confined to their houses throughout the long winter by ice and snow, had more reason to be gloomy and introspective than people in Mediterranean countries, who could get out into (16) .... sun all the year round. It is even reasonable to suppose that when the long summer evenings come to Norway and Sweden, with eighteen hours of daylight, the people have more excuse to celebrate by going a little mad and getting drunk.

Where the theory is generally accepted is in the comparisons made in almost every country in Europe between people from the north and the south. In England, southerners have always regarded those from the north as hard-working, but unpleasantly direct in speech and mean about money, while the northerners see Londoners, in particular, as lazy, self-indulgent and insincere. Anyone who goes to Milan or Barcelona will find people making the same criticisms of southerners from Naples or Seville and being condemned by them in the same way. Everywhere the warmer weather in the south seems to have produced the same contrast. Greece is a smaller country, with less scope for climatic differences and in ancient times, it was the Spartans, from the south, who were by tradition tougher and less pleasure-loving. Is Greece an exception to the general rule?

2 In the first three paragraphs, *the, a* or *an* have been left out in some cases. Study *Reference section I* on page 64 and *Reference section 13* on page 69. Now complete the essay by writing *a/an* or *the* only where necessary.

3 Answer these questions.

a In what ways did Toynbee think climate affected people?

....

b Why is this generalisation not always applicable?

....

c What makes it seem logical in some cases?

....

d In what context is it generally accepted to be true in many countries?

....

e Why is this less logical than the comparison made in paragraph 3?

....

4 Read these questions and write an essay on one of them.

a Your tutor shows you two extracts from articles about personality traits.

> *Courage is the greatest virtue. If you are not brave, the rest are no use. In this day and age, there is no place for the faint-hearted.*

> *Nowadays, it appears that the only thing which will help us survive is our sense of humour. There's absolutely no point in being conscientious when all around you are slacking off. The main thing is that you are able to laugh things off.*

Your tutor asks you to write an essay about the most important personality trait in today's world responding to the points raised and giving your own views on the matter. Write your essay.

You can prepare for this choice by completing these exercises first.

Put the following virtues in ranking order. Write a number from 1 to 7 in the space provided.

courage   ....   honesty   ....   generosity   ....   a sense of humour   ....
hard work   ....   chastity   ....   humility   ....

Use your answers to these questions to help you come up with a plan for the composition.

1 Do we judge people by one virtue alone or a combination?
....

2 Nevertheless, some virtues are more important than others. Which ones and why?
....

3 How do you rate courage and humour against the others you have mentioned?
....

4 How accurate do you think the extracts are?
....

b Your tutor shows you two extracts from articles about personal happiness.

> *While it is true to say that money can't buy you happiness, you can't be happy without it. How can anyone be expected to be happy with their lot if they haven't got anything? Without the basic necessities, it is unrealistic to expect to be happy.*

> *There is nothing more important in the world than one's health. Without it, one's life is at best uncomfortable, at worst a complete misery. One cannot be expected to be happy if in pain, or if one's friends or family are ill. Therefore, the only guarantee to happiness is one's health.*

Your tutor asks you to write an essay about personal happiness responding to the points raised and giving your own views on the matter. Write your essay.

Consider the points made in the extracts in a four-paragraph plan, like this:

1 Short introduction, indicating your opinion
2 If money does not make people happy, what does? Define what you think does make them happy.
3 Can the lack of money cause unhappiness and prevent people from enjoying life? Think of examples.
4 How far are the extracts true? To what extent does money contribute to happiness and how does it do so?

Tip

Most people would not immediately answer 'yes' or 'no' to questions like the ones in this unit. The best way to answer is to find something interesting to say, giving examples from what you know. Do not fill your essay with well-meaning generalisations.

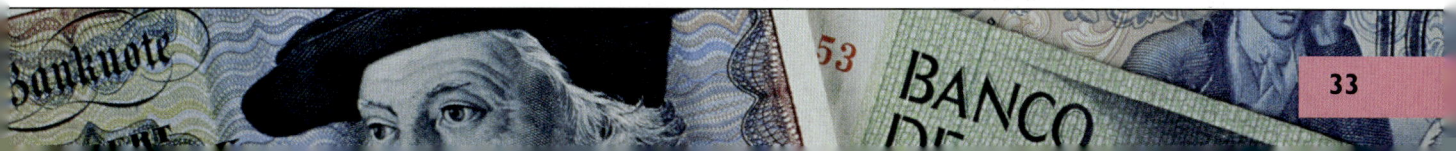

1 Read the question and the essay below and complete the exercises that follow.

You have attended a course on health and have been asked by your tutor to write an essay on the importance of diet to good health. You have been to a lecture on the subject and have made the notes below. Write your essay using your notes and expressing your own opinions.

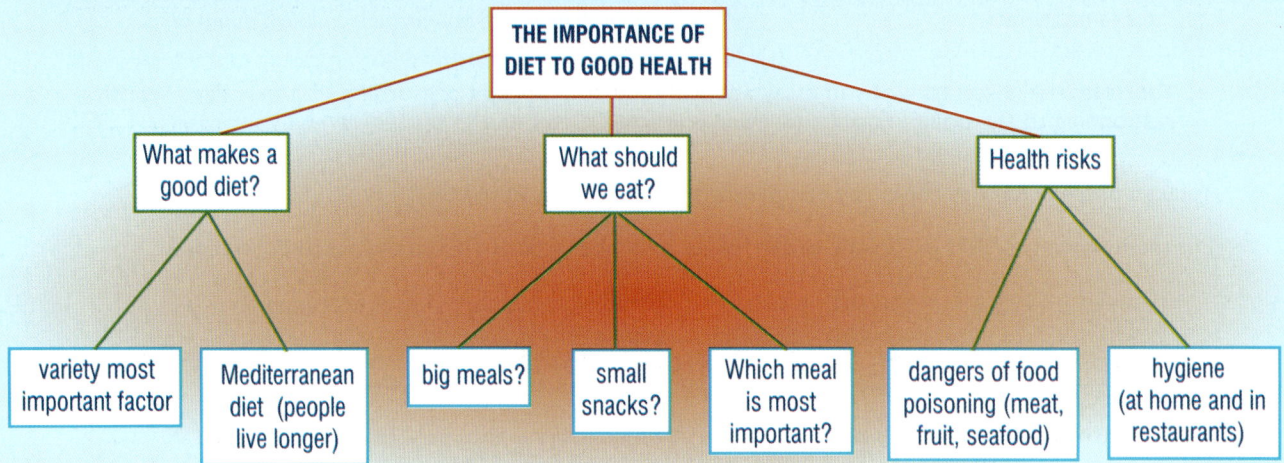

```
                    THE IMPORTANCE OF
                    DIET TO GOOD HEALTH

        What makes a         What should         Health risks
         good diet?           we eat?

  variety most    Mediterranean   big meals?   small    Which meal   dangers of food    hygiene
  important       diet (people                 snacks?  is most      poisoning (meat,   (at home and in
  factor          live longer)                          important?   fruit, seafood)    restaurants)
```

(1) .... that diet is essential to good health. Choosing the right diet, (2) .... , depends on a number of factors. (3) .... , what we eat is obviously important. (4) .... , we need to consider how often we have a meal and which meals should be the main meals of the day. (5) .... , even if our diet is suitable, we must do our best to ensure that the food we eat is not contaminated.

Even the experts disagree about what constitutes the best diet. There is, (6) ...., fairly general agreement that a balanced diet like the 'Mediterranean diet', mainly consisting of fruit, vegetables and fish but also including some meat, is the healthiest and, (7) ...., people who follow it live longer. The key to a good diet is really variety. In places where people depend entirely on one kind of food, their diet will lack some vitamins and their health will suffer.

We may have our main meal during the day or in the evening but there is no doubt that it is better to have a good breakfast than eat a lot late at night. We need energy at the beginning of a day's work but not when going to bed, when a big meal may lead to indigestion. Regular meals are also important. Young people often get indigestion because they eat sweets, cakes and fast food in between meals and have no appetite when they go home for lunch or dinner.

(8) ...., the right diet does not always prevent illness, though we can minimise the risks by insisting on cleanliness in restaurants and refusing to eat anything that is not quite fresh. Some diseases contracted by animals may be passed to human beings eating meat; insecticides sprayed on fruit trees may be poisonous if we eat the fruit raw; some coastal waters are contaminated and seafood caught there can cause food poisoning. In normal circumstances, however, the right diet is the essential factor for good health. It can make us strong, keep our weight down and so enable us to live longer.

2 Study *Connectors and Modifiers* on page 70 and complete the essay above with the phrases below.

apart from that	*as a result*	*however*	*in the first place*
it goes without saying	*nevertheless*	*finally*	*of course*

3   Essays providing information generally make a number of main points, contained in topic sentences. These are usually supported by examples or explanation. Find the main points in the essay opposite and the sentences that support them. The first has been done for you.

a   Paragraph 1: One main point followed by examples.

 Main point: Choosing the right diet depends on a number of factors.

 Examples: the three sentences that follow

b   Paragraph 2: One main point, followed by a sentence of explanation.

....

....

c   Paragraph 3: Two main points, each followed by explanation or example.

....

....

....

....

d   Paragraph 4: Two main points, one followed by examples, the other by a comment.

....

....

....

....

4   Look at the question below and then do the exercises.

You have attended a talk about alternative medicine and the value of homeopathic remedies in particular, and have made the notes below. Your tutor has now asked you to write an essay on this subject using your notes.

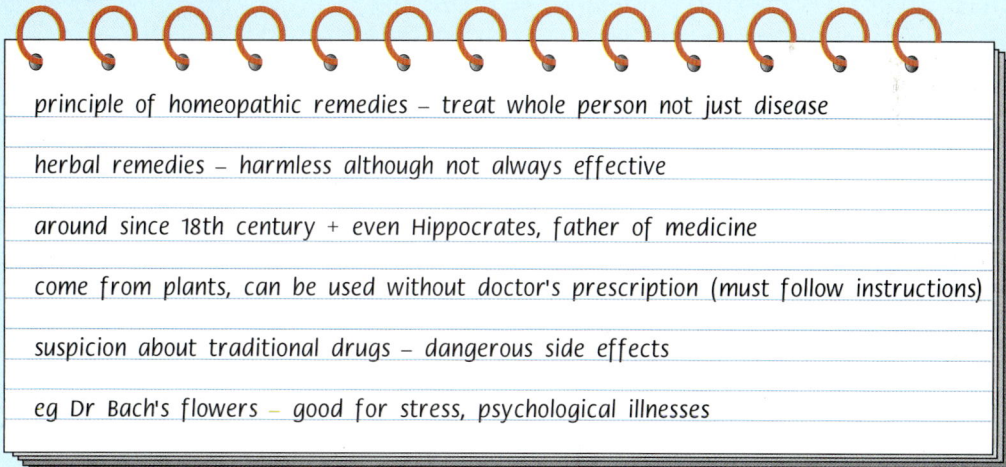

 principle of homeopathic remedies – treat whole person not just disease

 herbal remedies – harmless although not always effective

 around since 18th century + even Hippocrates, father of medicine

 come from plants, can be used without doctor's prescription (must follow instructions)

 suspicion about traditional drugs – dangerous side effects

 eg Dr Bach's flowers – good for stress, psychological illnesses

a   Why are people turning to homeopathic remedies?   ....

b   What is the advantage of using them?   ....

c   What example of a homeopathic remedy is given?   ....

d   What is it used for?   ....

e   How long have homeopathic remedies been in use?   ....

f   What principle is behind homeopathic remedies?   ....

g   What are they made from?   ....

h   What precautions must you take if you use them to treat yourself?   ....

5 Read Lucy's essay to see how she has organised the information from her notes into paragraphs.

In (1) .... recent years, many people have become suspicious of (2) .... traditional drugs prescribed by their doctors because they have read that (3) .... number of them have (4) .... dangerous side effects. As (5) .... result, they are turning to (6) .... alternative medicine and (7).......... homeopathy.

(8) .... herbal remedies have (9) .... advantage of being harmless, even if they do not always cure (10) .... disease (11) .... patient is suffering from. (12) .... example of one such remedy is (13) .... Dr Bach's flowers, which are supposed to have (14) .... special properties helping (15) .... people to overcome (16) .... symptoms of (17) .... stress and (18) .... similar psychological illnesses.

(19) .... homeopathy is essentially (20) .... natural healing process, stimulating (21) .... body's natural forces to (22) .... recovery. (23) .... remedies used are generally obtained from (24) .... plants. They are available to treat (25) .... wide range of (26) .... illnesses and can be used without (27) .... consulting (28) .... doctor, provided (29) .... patient chooses (30) .... right cure, (31) .... cure that matches his symptoms, and he follows (32) .... instructions for (33) .... use very carefully.

Although (34) .... turn towards (35) .... alternative medicine would seem to be (36) .... recent phenomenon, in fact, (37) .... homeopathic remedies (38) .... people use today have been in (39) .... existence since (40) .... eighteenth century. (41) .... principle behind them is even older and derives from Hippocrates, (42) .... father of (43) .... medicine, who recognised that it is necessary to treat (44) .... whole person, and not just (45) .... disease he is suffering from.

6 *A/an* and *the* have been left out of Lucy's essay. Add them only where necessary.

7   Choose one of the questions below and write an essay.

a   You have been asked by your tutor to write an essay on the importance of exercise to good health. Write your essay using the notes below and expressing your own ideas.

```
              THE IMPORTANCE OF
              EXERCISE TO GOOD HEALTH

   What is a good          What exercise              Health risks
 exercise programme?      should we do?

 interesting    regular      low impact   high impact      heart      obesity
and enjoyable  exercise                                   disease
```

b   You attended a lecture on the subject of addictions and the threat they pose to good health. Your tutor has asked you to write an essay on the subject using the notes opposite and expressing your own ideas.

can take many forms: alcohol, smoking, taking drugs, work

all can be dangerous to your health

some are deadly: lung cancer, cirrhosis of the liver

passive smoking

pregnant women can pass their drug addiction on to their unborn baby

are started by peer pressure, stress/anxiety, curiosity

difficult to quit – special support groups & rehabilitation programmes (eg Alcoholics Anonymous)

1 Read through the question and the proposal below to get a general idea of the meaning and then complete the exercises that follow.

> You are a member of a sports club and have been asked by the club to write a proposal to the local authorities asking for financial help to develop the first aid facilities currently available at the sports centre. It has been suggested that you focus on existing facilities, what exactly is required and how the funds would benefit those people using the sports centre. Write your proposal.

....

This proposal aims to outline the reasons why funding is required by the Five Oaks Sports Centre in order to improve first aid facilities available at the centre. It will also show that these improvements are necessary and will benefit members.

....

Currently the first aid provisions at the centre are insufficient. There is a first aid box in the reception area and a qualified member of staff is on duty to deal with minor injuries and accidents. Unfortunately this member of staff has other duties to perform during working hours and is not always easy to locate. Valuable time could be lost trying to track down the individual in the event of an accident of a more serious nature. This is obviously an undesirable situation that needs to be corrected.

....

In the event that funding is made available, the first priority is the creation of a first aid station within the sports centre. This would need to be clearly signposted so people can find it quickly and easily, and fully equipped with the necessary supplies. Secondly, the appointment of qualified, full-time members of staff employed to work within the station is also necessary. There would only need to be one on duty at any one time although other employees who have some first aid training could be on call should they be required. These members of staff would need to be be supplied with beepers, so they could be contacted at any time regardless of where there may be. Finally, telephones connected directly to the first aid centre should be installed to enable people requiring assistance at the site of an accident to phone for that assistance.

....

At present those people using the sports centre who suffer an injury or become unwell are not being properly catered for. If the suggestions above were implemented, fast and effective assistance would be readily available at all times. This would benefit our members and the public who use the centre, increasing the confidence that people have in the Five Oaks Sports Centre.

2 Choose the best heading for each paragraph, write the numbers 1-4 on the dotted lines below, and write the headings in the spaces in the proposal.

a How funding would be spent   ....
b Purpose   ....
c Existing facilities   ....
d Benefits   ....

3   Now look at the proposal again and answer these questions.

a   What are the two shortcomings of the first aid facilities currently provided by the Five Oaks Sports Centre?

....

b   How many suggestions does the proposal include?

....

c   What are these suggestions?

....

4   Below is a table listing four different kinds of proposal. With a partner, look at the list of shortcomings and benefits in the box. Can you complete the table with the missing information?

advice on retraining, re-entering the job market	no local computer facilities except Internet cafés
allow access for local community as well as students	no quiet area for study
hold inter-college games	occupy children
inadequate facilities, old/damaged equipment	reference section – homework, research
Internet access	school leavers – further education
no childcare facilities	the unemployed – training/job opportunities
limited sports facilities shared with public	no help/advice for school leavers, the unemployed or
mothers/fathers free to shop	people wanting to return to work

Proposal	Existing shortcomings	Benefits
provide funds to create a study area & town library with computers	1 .... 2	1 .... 2 .... 3 work on own
funds for baby minding / childcare service in large shopping centre	1 .... (children bored – misbehave, shops difficult to navigate with pushchairs, young children, etc)	1 .... 2 ....
funds for career advisory service	1	1 .... 2 .... 3 ....
funds for improving sports facilities for college/community	1 .... 2	1 .... 2 .... 3 meet people

5 A proposal needs to be written in a formal style. Look at these sentences below and tick (✓) those that you think would be suitable to include in a proposal.

1 I think that a place where mums and dads can leave their kids for an hour or two is a really good idea.   ....

2 Unfortunately, the sports facilities available are inadequate and much of the equipment is either old or damaged.   ....

3 Lots of people don't want to sit in a smoky, noisy café just so they can surf the net.   ....

4 This proposal tries to say why our town needs a career advisory service.   ....

5 The provision of such a service would leave parents free to shop in the knowledge that their children are being well looked after.   ....

6 I'm sure you'll agree that a computer and study area is just what our town library needs.   ....

7 If the sports centre is really good and cheap, lots of people will use it.   ....

8 This proposal outlines the reasons why Upper Cheston requires funding to create a Careers Advisory Service that would be of benefit to local people of all ages.   ....

6 Can you rewrite the sentences from exercise 5 that you did not tick, so they are in a more suitable style?

a ....
....
....

b ....
....
....

c ....
....
....

d ....
....
....

e ....
....
....

7 Choose one of the questions below and write a proposal, using the information from exercises 4-6 to help you.

a You work at the local library and you and your colleagues have decided to ask the local authority for funding to extend the services offered. The funding would be used to create a quiet study/reading area and provide a computer area where members of the public would be able to use the computers and also access the Internet. Write a proposal outlining why these facilities are necessary and how they would benefit the community as a whole.

b You are a qualified child minder and have decided to write a proposal applying for funds to start up your own business. You would like to use the money to provide childcare facilities at a shopping centre in the nearby town. It has been suggested that you include details of the lack of facilities presently available, how you would spend the money and how your plans would be of benefit.

c You are a youth counsellor and have been asked to write a proposal to the local authority asking for funds to create a careers advisory service in your town. You should explain why this service is needed and how it would benefit the community.

d You are a member of the Student Union at your university. There have been a number of complaints about the lack of sports facilities available to students and it has been decided that the university will apply to the local authority for funds to make improvements. You have been asked to write a proposal outlining the existing facilities and explaining how the money should be spent.

1 Read the question and the proposal below and complete the exercises that follow.

> You have read a notice in the local newspaper from the town council inviting residents to give their opinions on how money raised at a recent fair could be used. The town councillors have made some suggestions – extending the town library, improving the local park or renovating a local building. You decide to send in a proposal, commenting on these possibilities, and stating which idea would be the best for the local community and why.

Purpose
The aim of this proposal is to discuss the suggestions which were made by the town councillors on how the money raised at the 1st Annual Summer Fair should best be spent.

Town Library
The town library, which is very popular with the local residents and is said to be one of the best in the country, is very cramped, with space being at a premium. This is partly due to the fact that the new audio section occupies a (1) .... amount of space in the main library, which means that the wide variety of books available has to be crammed into a much smaller space than would otherwise be desirable. It is, therefore, logical that some people feel that building an extension would be a (2) .... way to spend the money raised at the Summer Fair.

St Leonard's Park
The park on St Leonard's Street has long been a meeting place for old and young alike. However, with the exception of the gardens, which are very well cared for, the park is (3) .... in need of repair. The open-air stage, which was once the venue for many plays and concerts, has been badly vandalised, and a (4) .... amount of money will be needed in order that it be restored. Furthermore, the children's playground is, for want of a better word, a safety hazard, and this must be rectified immediately if the town council is to avoid being held accountable for accidents.

The Old Schoolhouse
For many years now, there has been talk about the renovation of the old schoolhouse in the main town square. Unfortunately, this has not yet been brought to fruition. It is (5) .... a great pity that this building, which is part of our local heritage, has been allowed to fall into disrepair. However, the cost of renovating such a building would (6) .... exceed the funds available at this time.

Recommendation
In conclusion, while all three suggestions would benefit the local community in some way, it is my belief that St Leonard's Park deserves our (7) .... attention. I hope that the points outlined in this proposal will receive your (8) .... consideration.

2 Read the proposal again and fill the gaps using the adjectives and adverbs below. More than one answer may be possible.

badly	commendable	considerable	immediate
serious	substantial	surely	undoubtedly

3   Find words and phrases in the proposal which mean the same as:

a   limited   ....

b   takes up   ....

c   really needs mending   ....

d   fixed   ....

e   blamed for   ....

f   carried out   ....

g   deteriorate in condition ....

h   be more than   ....

4   Answer these questions about the proposal on the previous page.

a   In which paragraph does the writer state the purpose of the proposal?
....

b   In which paragraph does the writer state which of the suggestions he thinks is the best?
....

c   What does the writer do in the first sentences in paragraphs 3-5?
....

d   What are the main reasons for spending money on each of the suggestions?

Town Library: ....
St Leonard's Park: ....
The Old Schoolhouse: ....

e   Underline the explanations/examples given for the reasons. Are there explanations/examples for all three suggestions? Why do you think this is?
....
....
....

f   Put the three suggestions in order, starting with the one the writer thinks is the most appropriate, writing the words from the proposal which helped you find your answer.
....
....
....

5 Look at the sentences below. They are written in the active voice. In the proposal, find corresponding sentences in the passive voice and write them below.

Tip

As with all formal writing, the passive voice is used in proposals. This is mainly due to the fact that it is not appropriate to talk directly to the person who is going to read the proposal. This is especially true if blame is being apportioned.

a The aim of this proposal is to discuss the suggestions which the town councillors made.

....

b They say that the town library is one of the best in the country.

....

c They have to cram the wide variety of books available into a much smaller place.

....

d Someone has badly vandalised the open-air stage, which was once the venue for many plays and concerts.

....

e You will need a considerable amount of money in order that it be restored.

....

f You must rectify this immediately if the town council is to avoid someone holding them responsible for accidents.

....
....

6 Rewrite the following sentences using the passive voice where possible.

a Someone must hire a bus when the hockey team plays away from home.
....

b Unfortunately, we will not raise a lot of money for the field trip.
....

c They said that the science lab at this college is the best in the country.
....

d Someone needs to look after the employees' children while employees are working.
....

e   They should buy a cooker or a microwave oven for people to heat up food.

....

f   You could set up a gym in the basement, which nobody uses.

....

7   Write a proposal on one of the following questions. Do the exercises before you begin writing to help you.

a   Your college has been given funding by a famous former student and the Student Committee has made some suggestions – a new science lab, a new mini-bus or a field trip abroad. You decide to send in a proposal, commenting on these possibilities, and stating which idea would be the best and why.

Answer the following questions to complete the paragraph plan.

Introduction:	What is the aim of your proposal?
	....
Paragraph 2:	What reason and explanation/example can you think of for building a new science lab?
	....
Paragraph 3:	What reason and explanation/example can you think of for a new mini-bus?
	....
Paragraph 4:	What reason and explanation/example can you think of for a field trip abroad?
	....
Conclusion:	What is your recommendation?
	....

b   The company you work for has been given funding to improve working conditions. The board of directors has made three suggestions – childcare facilities, cooking facilities or building a gym. Employees have been asked to send in proposals commenting on these possibilities, stating which idea would be the best and why. Write your proposal.

Answer the following questions to complete the paragraph plan.

Introduction:	What is the aim of your proposal?
	....
Paragraph 2:	What reason and explanation/example can you think of for childcare facilities?
	....
Paragraph 3:	What reason and explanation/example can you think of for cooking facilities?
	....
Paragraph 4:	What reason and explanation/example can you think of for a building a gym?
	....
Conclusion:	What is your recommendation?
	....

I Read the question and the proposal below and do the exercises that follow.

You are a member of the local tourist association which recently held a meeting on the problem of the reduction in the number of visitors to the area. You attended the meeting and have been asked to write a proposal for the local authorities evaluating the situation and making some recommendations, using the notes you took at the meeting.

Problem:
drop in tourism – 30% in 5 yrs
hotels, restaurants and shops had to shut down
10% more people out of work

Solutions:
1   advertising
2   clean up beaches
3   appeal to different tourists

Purpose

The purpose of this proposal is to discuss the problems the local tourist industry faces and to put forward measures that could be taken to improve the situation.

Current Situation

Unfortunately, our town is confronted by the same problem that is crippling the rest of the country. The fall in the number of tourists visiting our town is having a devastating impact on the local community. In just five years, local tourism has declined by 30%, forcing many businesses to close. As a result, local unemployment has increased by 10%. Outlined below are some suggestions that could help rectify this situation.

Recommendations

1   Many of our members feel that the key to increasing local tourism is to diversify into other kinds of tourism. Perhaps the local council should consider different ways of promoting our town as a holiday resort by providing financial assistance to those who wish to invest in our area. If grants were given to investors to set up new ventures, such as specialist holiday companies, there would be more variety which would encourage different sorts of tourists to visit our area.

2   In order to attract visitors to our area, it is essential that we have attractive beaches and coastlines. This would entail clearing beaches of rubbish, and making sure that all beach bars and seaside restaurants are attractive to look at, unlike some of the monstrosities which are spoiling the coastline at present. Providing this measure is taken, the visitors who come here on beach holidays would be encouraged to return, and our reputation as a beach resort would improve.

3   Another answer to the problem would be to launch an international advertising campaign. If local government funds were made available for such a campaign, the local tourist association would do its utmost to make a sizable contribution. This would be an excellent way to promote the region and encourage tourism. Had we done this earlier, we may have been able to avoid the unfortunate situation in which we find ourselves today.

Conclusion

It is imperative that something is done to ensure the revival of local tourism. It is our firm conviction that the implementation of the suggestions above would make a significant contribution to this.

2 Find words and phrases in the proposal which are similar in meaning to the ones below. Sometimes more than one answer is possible.

a reduction ....

b faces ....

c local community ....

d making ....

e shut down ....

f 10% more people are out of work ....

g make recommendations ....

h cleaning up beaches ....

> **Tip**
>
> *Don't use the same words and phrases in your writing that are in the question. Try to use synonyms, or paraphrase as far as possible.*

3 Read the question and the proposal again and answer the following questions.

In which paragraph(s) does the writer:

a describe the general situation at the time of writing? ....

b make a recommendation based on information given in the notes? ...., ... and ....

c state that the aim of the proposal is to evaluate the situation and make recommendations? ....

d state that your recommendations will help improve the situation? ....

e explain how the recommendation can be implemented? ...., ... and ....

f rephrase the information about the problem given in the notes? ....

g state the importance of measures being taken? ....

h explain what the result of the recommendation will be? ...., ... and ....

> **Tip**
>
> *In proposals like this one, you are trying to persuade someone to take action. Therefore, you should do your best to make them understand how important something is.*

4 Rewrite the sentences below using the words in bold. Use between two and five words. You may wish to look back at the model for help with the structures needed.

a The fact that business is bad is having a huge effect on the local community.
devastating
The lack of business .... on the local community.

b Many people feel that giving grants to new businesses is the way to increase trade.
key
Many people feel that the .... to give grants to new businesses.

c The authorities might like to think about ways to tidy up the neighbourhood.
consider
Perhaps the authorities .... cleaning up the neighbourhood.

d Unemployed people must be trained properly if we are to reduce the unemployment level.
essential
In order to reduce the unemployment level, ... people are trained properly.

e This is how best to encourage business in the area.
excellent
This .... to encourage business in the area.

f We must do something before it's too late.
imperative
It .... done before it is too late.

5 Look at *Reference section 4a, b* and *e* on pages 64-65 and *Reference section 11* on page 67 and then complete the proposal below with the correct form of the verbs in brackets or using *would* where necessary.

You are head editor of the college newspaper and you recently attended a staff meeting about the problem of low readership. You have been asked to write a proposal for the Principal evaluating the situation and outlining some suggestions, using the notes you took at the staff meeting.

Problem:
college wants to stop publishing
college newspaper not popular enough
local advertisers want to pull out

Solutions:
1 make appearance more up-to-date
2 make available in other areas of college
3 special features on local events

Purpose
The purpose of this proposal is to discuss the problems the college newspaper faces and to make recommendations which (1) .... (improve) the situation.

Current Situation
Unfortunately, our newspaper is in grave danger of being closed down. The college is seriously considering withdrawing its funding, on the grounds that circulation is not high enough. Furthermore, local advertisers are contemplating withdrawing from the newspaper for the same reason. Outlined below are some suggestions that (2) .... (help) rectify this situation.

Recommendations
1 In order to increase the circulation of the college newspaper, it is imperative that there are a number of points of sale apart from the English Department, where it is sold at present. This (3) .... (entail) persuading other members of staff on the newspaper to give up some of their time in order to sell papers at the main college entrance. The Students' Union (4) .... (be) another suitable location. (5) .... (this/think of) sooner, we may already have been making a profit.

2 Some members of staff believe that the key to increasing circulation is to bring the newspaper into the 21st century. Perhaps the design department could create a new concept for the paper. If the newspaper looked more modern, students (6) .... (undoubtedly find) it more attractive.

3 Another answer to the problem would be to have new features and articles which students want to find out about. For example, a 'What's On' section could be included, with details of local cinemas, concerts, etc. This (7) .... (be) an excellent way to encourage students to buy the newspaper on a regular basis.

Conclusion
It is vital that something is done to prevent the college newspaper being closed down. If suggestions such as the ones above (8) .... (take) seriously, we believe that the newspaper can be saved.

6 Read the question and the proposal again and complete the paragraph plan.

Introduction:
Aim? .... *discuss newspaper's problems and suggest improvements* ....

Current Situation:
General situation? ....
Information about the problem? ....

Recommendations:

Recommendation 1? ....
How to implement? ....
Result? ....

Recommendation 2? ....
How to implement? ....
Result? ....

Recommendation 3? ....
How to implement? ....
Result? ....

Conclusion:
State the importance of measures being taken.
State that your recommendations will improve the situation.

7 Now write the following proposal using the notes below.

You are a member of the local business people's association which recently held a meeting on the problem of the lack of business in the area. You attended the meeting and have been asked to write a proposal for the local authorities evaluating the situation and outlining some suggestions, using the notes you took at the meeting.

Problem:
business is bad – down 25% in 3 yrs
more and more businesses are closing
area almost deserted
unemployment up

Solutions:
1 tidy up area
2 training for the unemployed – old and
   young alike
3 grants for new business people

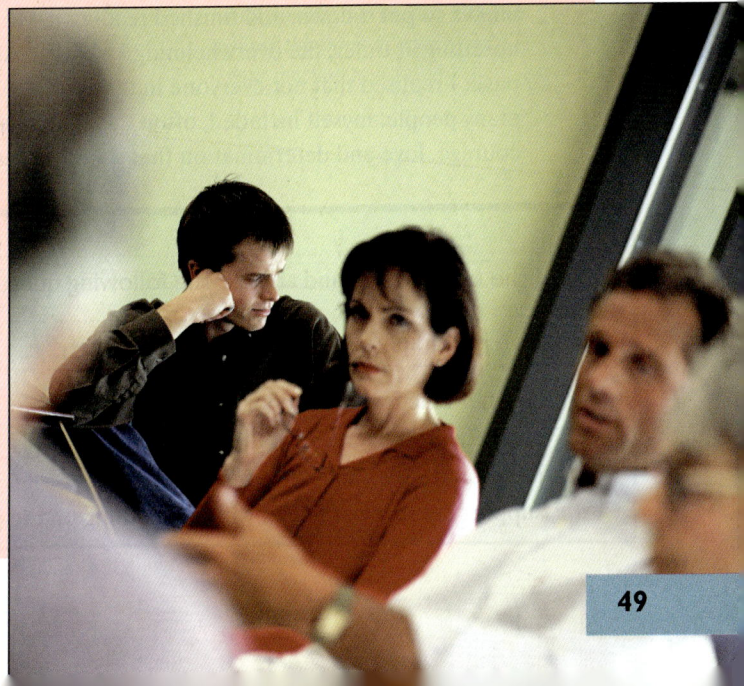

Reference Section

1   *A an*

An is used before a vowel sound: **an** elephant, **an** umbrella, **an** aeroplane; but not when **u** is pronounced like '**you**': **a u**seful book. It is also used before **h** when **h** is not pronounced: **an h**onest man.

When we mention something for the first time, we normally use **a/an**; when that thing is referred to again, we use the definite article **the**, because by now it is understood which one we mean:
A photographer took his photograph without permission. He got so angry that he broke **the photographer's** camera.

We also use **a/an** in numerical expressions (for example, in expressions of frequency or quantity):
She has classes three times a week.
Petrol costs about sixty pence a litre here.
(See also **the**, **use and omission**)

2   Adjectives

a   Position

1   Adjectives generally come before the noun or as a complement after **be** and some other verbs (**look**, **seem**, **feel** etc.)
*She's a **pretty** girl. She **looks** very **pretty**.*

2   When we use more than one adjective before a noun we do not usually write **and** between the adjectives. We use commas if the combination is not usual, but not if it is very common. Compare:
*He's a **nice little** man.* (common)
*She's a **shy, secretive** woman.* (not usual)
We use **and** when the adjectives are a complement after **be**, **seem**, **feel**, etc.:
*He's **short and fat**./She seems **charming and intelligent**.*
With three adjectives, we usually put a comma after the first:
*We were **cold, wet** and **tired**.*

b   Order

In normal usage, we prefer to put some adjectives before others:
*He's a **nice little** man* (NOT *little nice*).
The rule is that general adjectives like **nice** or **pretty** come before more precise ones. Note these examples:
a   *I've read the **first hundred** pages.* (ordinal–cardinal)

b   *An **intelligent young** man* (mental ability–age)
c   *A **large round** ball* (size–shape)
d   *A **green cotton** dress* (colour–material)
e   *A **German car** factory* (nationality/origin–purpose)

c   Compound adjectives

Compound adjectives are sometimes made with an adjective and a noun plus an **-ed** ending. The meaning is usually **with** or **having**:
*He's a **red-haired, broad-shouldered** man.*
*(He's a man with **red hair** and **broad shoulders**.)*

3   Adverbs of frequency

a   Adverbs of frequency, like **always** and **often** and other single-word adverbs of indefinite time like **recently**, generally go before the main verb but after forms of **be**:
*Margaret **is never** late; Jane **never comes** late, either.*

b   They usually go between an auxiliary and the main verb or after the first auxiliary if there are two or more:
*I **have never seen** such a good film.*
*She **must sometimes have wondered** if she had made the right decision.*

4   Conditional sentences

a   Present and future

We generally use the present tense for the condition and a future tense for the main clause, but note the alternative with the imperative:
***If** I **see** him tomorrow, I'll **give** him your message.*
***If** you **see** him tomorrow, **give** him my message.*

Modals may also be used in the main clause:
***If** you **go** out, you **must put on** your coat. It's cold.*

b   Imaginary situations in present or future

We use the past tense for the condition and the conditional tense (**would** + infinitive) for the main clause. With the verb **be**, we usually use **were** for all persons:
***If** I **were** (was) rich, I'**d buy** a house by the sea.*
***If** we **offered** you the job, **would** you **accept** it?*

c   Past situations

In talking about the past, we usually use the past perfect tense for the condition and the conditional perfect (**would have** + past participle) for the main clause:

*If I'**d known** what was wrong, I **would have told** you.*

But if the present situation is a direct result of an unfulfilled condition in the past, the main clause may be in the conditional tense:

*If I'**d studied** more when I was at school, I **would have** a better job today.*

d Permanent condition

If a condition is always true we use the present tense for both parts of the sentence:

*If it **doesn't rain**, the rivers **dry up** and the animals **die** of thirst.*

e Variations

1 As alternatives to **a** we can suggest that the possibility is not very likely:

*If you **should see** him, **will you give** him my message?* (please give him my message)

There is also a formal variation of this:

***Should** you **see** him, ...*

2 Alternatives to **b** are:

*If we **were to offer** you the job, **would** you **accept** it?*

***Were** we **to offer** you the job, ...*

These suggest that the offer is unlikely.

3 Alternatives to **c** are:

***Had** I **known**, I **would have informed** you.*

This is more formal than:

*If I **had known** ...*

5 Indirect questions: word order

In indirect questions, the question uses the affirmative or negative, not interrogative form: the word order is always subject before verb. If the direct question has no question word, the indirect question comes after **if/whether**; if it has a question word, this word is repeated in the indirect question:

*She wants to know **if/whether you are** English.*

*I wonder **where I will be** tomorrow.*

Note the changes in form in the present and past simple tenses:

*(Does he speak English?) Ask him **if/whether he speaks** English.*

*(What did he say?) I wonder **what he said**.*

If the question word is already the subject in the direct question, the word order will not change unless the verb is **be**:

*(What happened next?) Tell me **what happened** next.*

*(Who is she?) I wonder **who she is**.*

6 Indirect speech: paraphrase

Some verbs can be used in indirect speech to indicate the way things are said and the purpose of what was said. In the table below, note the purpose of the verb from the example in direct speech, and the constructions possible with the verbs we can use instead of **say** and **tell** in indirect speech:

Purpose	Verb	Direct speech and paraphrase
accusation	accuse	*'You stole it, didn't you?'* I accused **him of stealing** it.
admission	admit	*'Yes, I took it.'* He admitted **having taken** it.
advice	advise	*'You should take more exercise.'* He advised **her to take** more exercise. He advised **taking** more exercise.
agreement	agree	*'I think you're right.'* She agreed **with** me/the idea. *'All right. I'll help you'* She agreed **to help** me. *'That's the best method.'* We agreed **that it was** the best method. We agreed **on** the best method.
apology	apologise	*'I'm sorry I arrived late.'* He apologised **for arriving** late.
complaint	complain	*'You should have done the job better.'* He complained **that they should have** ... *'I wish he wouldn't do that.'* She complained **to me about him**.
denial	deny	*'I didn't steal it.'* He denied **that he had stolen** it. He denied **having stolen** it.
invitation	invite	*'Would you like to come to the party?'* He invited **her (to come)** to the party.
offer	offer	*'I'll help you, shall I?'* She offered **to help** me.
refusal	refuse	*'I won't do it.'* He refused **to do** it.
regret	regret	*'I wish I hadn't broken it.'* She regretted **having broken** it. She regretted **that she had broken** it.
reminder	remind	*'Don't forget to post it.'* She reminded **him to post** it.
suggestion	suggest	*'Why don't you go with her?'* He suggested **that I should** go with her. *'Let's go for a walk!'* She suggested **going** for a walk.
threat	threaten	*'If you don't go away, I'll call the police.'* He threatened **to call** the police if they didn't go away.
warning	warn	*'Be careful. The roads are icy.'* He warned **her to be** careful. He warned **her of/about** the icy roads. He warned her **that** the roads were icy.

7 Phrases in apposition

One way of giving additional information about a person or thing is to use a phrase in apposition (instead of a relative clause with a relative pronoun and a form of **be**).

Mr Taylor, (who is) **the team manager,** *said …*
The cathedral, (which is) **the oldest building in the city,** *was built …*

8 Prepositions of place

a *at, in, on*

At is used:
- for particular points: **at** *the end of the road,* **at** *number 27.*
- for places when we are concerned with their purpose or location, not their size or shape: **at** *the station,* **at** *the supermarket.*
  She works **at the post office.**
  (Compare: *She's* **in the post office,** *buying some stamps (= inside).)*
- for places (small towns, villages etc.) the speaker does not consider very important or does not know very well: **at Melton Mowbray,** *a town near Leicester. (Someone who lived there would probably say: I live* **in Melton Mowbray.)**

In suggests:
- 'inside' or a situation with three dimensions: **in the kitchen, in the High Street** (but USA = **on Main Street**) because of the houses on both sides.
- a large area, like a country, province, city: **in New Zealand, in Kent, in Manchester.**

On suggests:
- a surface: **on the wall, on Earth, on a small island.**
- a line: **on the coast, on the River Thames, on the road, on the way to …, on the left-hand side of the street.**

Also note the following:
They're sailing **in** *their boat* **on** *the lake.*
She's swimming **in** *the lake.*
In *the corner of the room (= inside)* but **at/on** *the corner of the street (= outside).*
He's **at** *the cinema (he's gone to see a film).*
I'll meet you **at** *the cinema. (outside, or near the door)*

They aren't here. They must be **in** *the cinema. (inside the building)*
On the screen *(surface),* **on the radio, on TV.**

b *into, onto, out of, off*

With verbs of movement, we generally use **into** and **onto,** though **in** and **on** are common:
He fell **into/in** *the water.*
He got **onto/on** *his bicycle.*

Out of indicates the opposite movement to **into** and **off** the opposite movement to **onto.** (See **in** and **on** in **a** above, for the idea of being 'inside' or 'on a surface'. Compare:
He took the knives and forks **out of** *the drawer.* (opposite of **into/in**)
We'll have to take the tyre **off** *the wheel.* (opposite of **onto/on**)

9 Prepositions of time

at, in, on
Use this list as a check:

- **at** for exact periods of time: **at five o'clock, at dinner time, at this moment.**
- **at** for festivals: **at Christmas, at Easter, at New Year.**
- others are: **at night** (but **during the day**), **at weekends, at present** (= now)

- **on** for days and dates: **on Monday, on June 10th, on Christmas Day** (compare **at** for the festive period), **on summer evenings, on Sunday morning, on Friday night**

- **in** for longer periods of time: **in August, in spring, in 1985, in the nineteenth century, in the Middle Ages, in the past, in the future** (compare **at present**)
- **in** for periods of time within which or at the end of which something may happen: **in the morning, in five minutes, in a week's time.**

10 Reported speech

a Statement

When we convert direct speech to reported speech and the introducing verb is in the past, the tense changes. Expressions of time and place also change unless the speaker is still in the same place on the same day (**here** is still **here,** and **today** is still **today**). Use the conversion table for reference and note that in all cases **told me** could replace **said**:

Direct	Reported
I'm **working** hard.	She said she **was working** hard.
I **travel** by train.	She said she **travelled** by train.
I'm **going to** change my job.	She said she **was going** to change …
I'll **see** you on Sunday.	She said she **would see** …
I've never **seen** it before.	She said she **had never seen** …
I **spoke** to him on Monday.	She said she **had spoken** …
I **can run** faster than him.	She said she **could run** …
The train **may arrive** late.	She said the train **might arrive** …
I **must go** to the doctor.	She said she **had to go** …
(with general future meaning)	She said she **would have to go** …

Other changes

here	there
this	that
now	then
yesterday	the day before, the previous day
tomorrow	the day after, the next day, the following day
last week	the week before, the previous week
next week	the week after, the next week, the following week
ago	before

b   Questions

Note the word order of indirect questions (see **Indirect questions**). The tense changes in reported questions are the same as for statements (see table in **a** above).

Direct	Reported
Have you **seen** the film?	She asked me **if** I **had seen** …
Where does he live?	She asked me **where** he **lived**.

c   Orders and requests

These are made with the imperative in direct speech. In reported speech we use the object + infinitive after **tell** (for orders) and **ask** (for requests):

Direct	Reported
Don't worry.	She **told him not to worry**.
Please **keep** quiet!	She **asked them to keep** quiet.

When we do not reproduce the actual words used in direct speech we can paraphrase what was said by using other verbs (**offer**, **suggest**, etc.) (See **Indirect speech: paraphrase**)

11   Should

a   should and ought to

Should and **ought to** indicate obligation or advice. We prefer **ought to** if we are doubtful that the obligation will be met or the advice will be taken:
You've got a bad cough. You **should/ought to** see a doctor.
You **ought to** see a doctor, but I don't suppose you will.

The past forms are **should/ought to have** + past participle. They are used to express regret in the first person, blame or criticism in the second and third:
I **shouldn't have said** that to her. It was very unkind. (regret)
You **should have been** more careful. Then you wouldn't have broken it. (blame or criticism)

b   Should and would

Should and **would** can both be used for the first person in the conditional tense, and as the past of **shall** for the first person in reported speech. But they have separate meanings and usage. (For **would** see Conditional sentences **4b**, **4c** and **4e**.)
Where they are often seen in combination is where sentences of advice or regret/blame (see **should a**) are followed by conditional sentences: They **shouldn't (should not) allow** motor cycles in the forest. If they kept them out, these fires **wouldn't (would not) start**.
You **should have taken** my advice. If you had, this **wouldn't (would not) have happened**.

CPE WRITING SHEETS

The writing sheets on the following pages have been specially designed for students to keep their work in an orderly fashion. Students should be encouraged to use the paragraph plans that are provided before writing their compositions.

It is recommended that all written work is kept in a folder. This makes it easier to refer back to earlier work at a later date, whether this is to monitor progress or for revision purposes.

Question

Introduction ....

Main Body ....

....

....

Conclusion ....

....
....
....
....
....
....
....
....
....
....
....
....
....
....
....
....
....
....
....
....
....
....
....
....
....
....
....

Question

Introduction	....
Main Body	....
	....
	....
Conclusion	....

....

....

....

....

....

....

....

....

....

....

....

....

....

....

....

....

....

....

....

....

....

....

....

....

....

....

Question

Introduction	....
Main Body	....
	....
	....
Conclusion	....

....

....

....

....

....

....

....

....

....

....

....

....

....

....

....

....

....

....

....

....

....

....

....

....

....

....

....

Question

Introduction ....

Main Body ....

....

....

Conclusion ....

....

....

....

....

....

....

....

....

....

....

....

....

....

....

....

....

....

....

....

....

....

....

....

....

....

Question

Introduction ....

Main Body ....

....

....

Conclusion ....

....

....

....

....

....

....

....

....

....

....

....

....

....

....

....

....

....

....

....

....

....

....

....

....

....

....

....

....

Question

Introduction	....
Main Body	....
	....
	....
Conclusion	....

....

....

....

....

....

....

....

....

....

....

....

....

....

....

....

....

....

....

....

....

....

....

....

....

....

....

....

Question

Introduction ....

Main Body ....

....

....

Conclusion ....

....

....

....

....

....

....

....

....

....

....

....

....

....

....

....

....

....

....

....

....

....

....

....

....

....

....

Question

Introduction	....
Main Body	....
	....
	....
Conclusion	....

....

....

....

....

....

....

....

....

....

....

....

....

....

....

....

....

....

....

....

....

....

....

....

....

Question

Introduction ....

Main Body ....
....
....

Conclusion ....

....
....
....
....
....
....
....
....
....
....
....
....
....
....
....
....
....
....
....
....
....
....
....
....

Question

Introduction ....
Main Body ....
....
....
Conclusion ....

....
....
....
....
....
....
....
....
....
....
....
....
....
....
....
....
....
....
....
....
....
....
....
....

Question

Introduction	....
Main Body	....
	....
	....
	....
Conclusion	....

....

....

....

....

....

....

....

....

....

....

....

....

....

....

....

....

....

....

....

....

....

....

....

....

....

....

....

Question

Introduction	....
Main Body	....
	....
	....
Conclusion	....

....
....
....
....
....
....
....
....
....
....
....
....
....
....
....
....
....
....
....
....
....
....
....
....
....
....

Question

Introduction	....
Main Body	....
	....
	....
Conclusion	....

....
....
....
....
....
....
....
....
....
....
....
....
....
....
....
....
....
....
....
....
....
....
....

Question

Introduction	....
Main Body	....
	....
	....
Conclusion	....

....
....
....
....
....
....
....
....
....
....
....
....
....
....
....
....
....
....
....
....
....
....
....
....
....